PLACES TO AND PEOPLE TO MEET IN IRELAND

Geography Books for Kids Age 9-12
Children's Explore the World Books

BABY PROFESSOR
EDUCATION KIDS

Speedy Publishing LLC

40 E. Main St. #1156

Newark, DE 19711

www.speedypublishing.com

Will you visit "The Emerald Isle"? That's Ireland, the second-largest island in Europe. If you get a chance to go there, who and what might you see? Let's find out!

A QUICK HISTORY OF IRELAND

Ireland is a land of rich green fields, good crops, and lots of livestock. But it also has rugged areas, lonely bogs, and steep cliffs leading down to the Atlantic Ocean.

The first people came to Ireland around 6,000 BCE, but we know little about them. By 3,000 BCE, people using stone tools were building farming communities.

Rock of Cashel

Around 700 BCE Celtic settlers began establishing villages and bases along Ireland's coast.

Viking's Hut

The next wave of of newcomers were Vikings. They first came as raiders, starting in the ninth century CE, but soon after established settlements. Some of their villages grew up to be large cities, like Dublin. Celts and Vikings fought each other for two hundred years, until a battle in 1014 showed the Celts would never push the Vikings out.

In 1170, invaders from England captured most of Ireland. When England became Protestant in the 1500s, Ireland remained Catholic. Much of the troubles the country has endured since have had a religious as well as a political basis.

A movement for Irish independence began in the 1820s and led to the creation of the Irish Free State, still within the British Empire, in 1922. In 1948, all but six counties became the independent country of Ireland. The six counties that remained part of Great Britain are mostly Protestant, and in the north-east of the island.

Northern Ireland Coast

Ireland was mainly agricultural into the 1900s. Many people emigrated to the United States and other countries during the great Potato Famine from 1845 to 1852. Learn more about the Irish in America in the Baby Professor book *Leprechaun In The US! The Story behind the St. Patrick's Day Celebration*.

Dublin with the Ha'penny Bridge

Today about five million people live in Ireland, and the country is home to huge software companies as well as traditional farms.

Many more millions overseas consider Ireland their homeland, even if they rarely get there.

GREAT CITY PLACES TO VISIT

There are many small cities in Ireland, each with its attractions. However only Dublin, the capital, has a population over one million. It makes sense, then, that a lot of the urban places to visit in Ireland are scattered around Dublin!

TRINITY COLLEGE

This is the oldest university in Ireland, founded in 1592. Some of its buildings date from before when the school was founded. Trinity College is a world of its own within Dublin, with cobbled streets and gorgeous architecture.

Students come from all around the world to learn and share their knowledge at Trinity College, and the library holdings include some remarkable early books. The college "Long Room" was the inspiration for the dining room at Hogwarts in the Harry Potter books and movies.

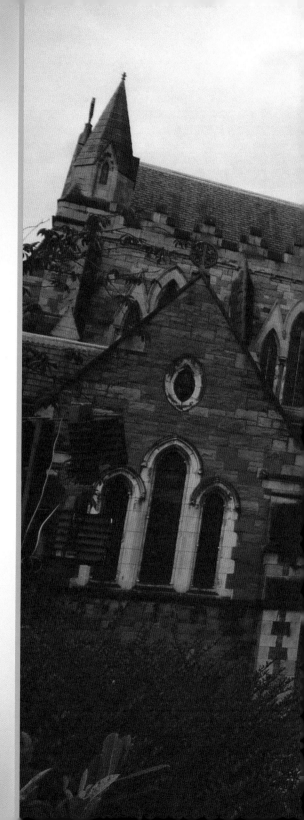

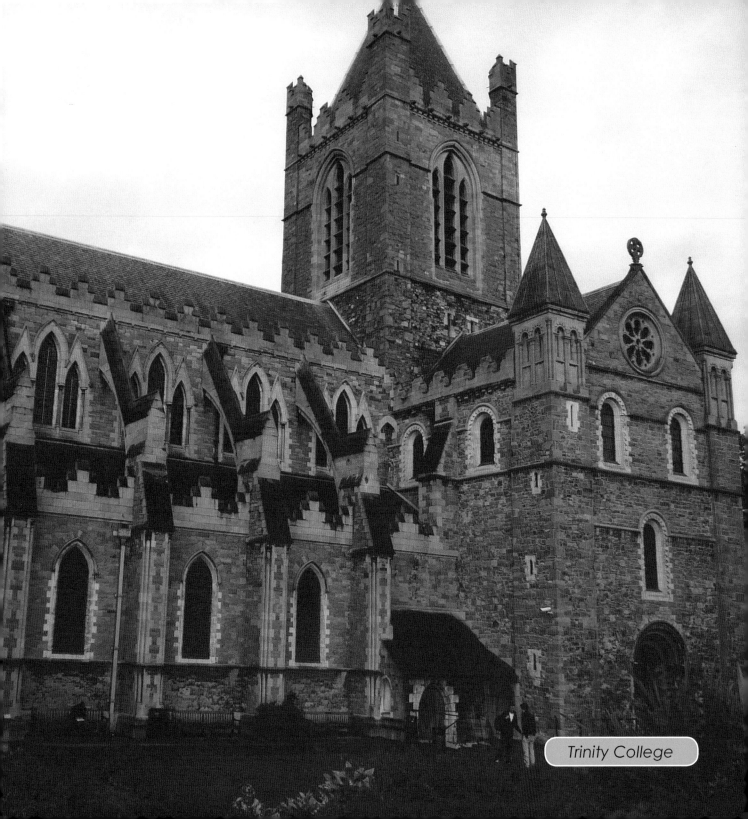

Trinity College

KILMAINHAM GAOL

This jail was built in 1796, and is a reminder that things have not always been green and friendly in Ireland. This is where the leaders of the independence uprising in 1916 were brought and, after being found guilty of high treason, were executed.

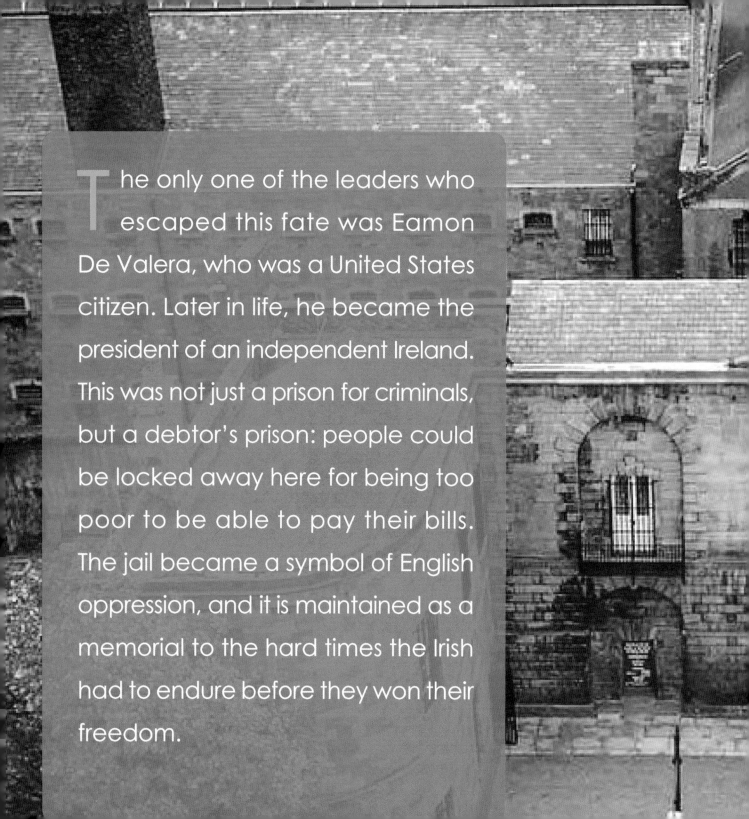

The only one of the leaders who escaped this fate was Eamon De Valera, who was a United States citizen. Later in life, he became the president of an independent Ireland. This was not just a prison for criminals, but a debtor's prison: people could be locked away here for being too poor to be able to pay their bills. The jail became a symbol of English oppression, and it is maintained as a memorial to the hard times the Irish had to endure before they won their freedom.

Kilmainham Gaol

ST. STEPHEN'S GREEN

This park is a welcome open space in the city, and is treasured by both Dubliners and tourists. You can sit and enjoy people-watching, have a picnic on the lawns, or feed the ducks. The ducks are so beloved that, during the independence uprising in 1916, the rebels and the government forces agreed to a daily truce around St. Stephen's Green so the park keepers could feed the ducks at the time of day they were used to.

St. Stephen's Green Park

St. Stephen's Green Park

Enjoy strolling the paths, watching the ducks in the Duck Pond, marveling at the stately trees, and taking in a soccer or hurley match on the sporting grounds. On the streets around "The Green" you can admire the Georgian architecture of the stately buildings. The Shelbourne Hotel, founded in 1824, is a great place to take afternoon tea.

B ut Ireland is not just Dublin. Beautiful people and places await you outside of town.

The Cliffs of Moher

THE CLIFFS OF MOHER

The cliffs stretch along the Atlantic coast for eight kilometers, less than two hours from the city of Galway. The views are wild and beautiful, and almost a million people come to see them every year.

MUCKROSS HOUSE AND GARDENS

This 19th-century estate in Killarney National Park hosted Queen Victoria for a visit. When you visit, you can see the sort of lifestyle the nobility of England and Ireland expected and enjoyed.

Nearby are farms worked in the traditional way, to give you an experience of how the majority of the country lived while the few enjoyed their gracious living in places like Muckross House.

Muckross House and Gardens

Stone Walls

THE ARAN ISLANDS

The people of the Aran Islands speak Gaelic as their first language, and preserve many old traditions that are different from the way of life you find in the rest of Ireland.

There are ancient stone forts and windswept cliffs to walk along. There are three islands, and each has delights of beautiful landscapes and people waiting for you.

THE RING OF KERRY

In county Kerry travel the Ring, a great scenic route around the Iveragh Peninsula. There are views of the Atlantic Ocean and wild mountains, and along the road are villages just waiting for you to take their picture.

The Ring of Kerry Coastline

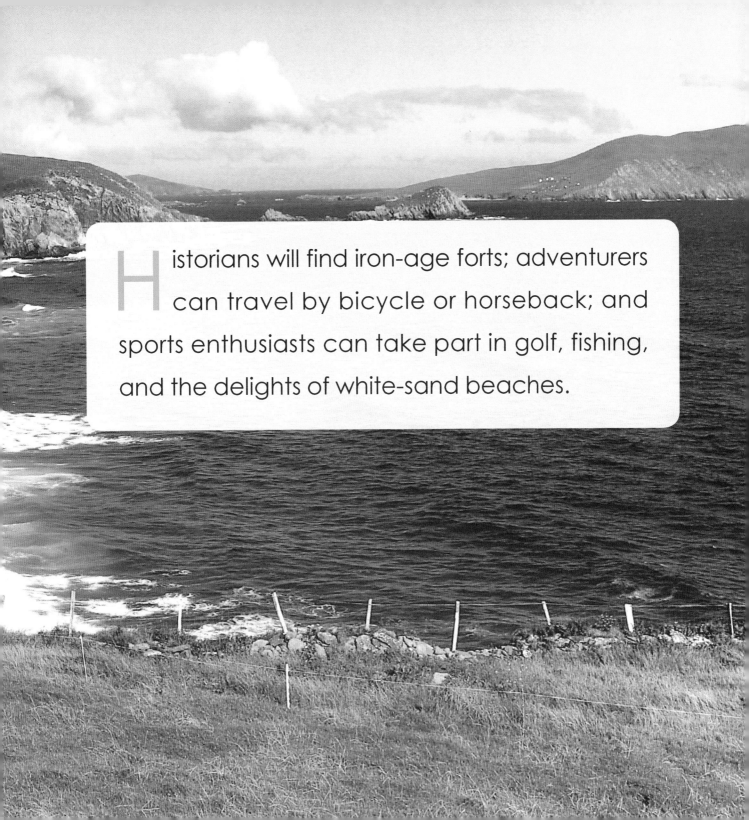

Historians will find iron-age forts; adventurers can travel by bicycle or horseback; and sports enthusiasts can take part in golf, fishing, and the delights of white-sand beaches.

BUNRATTY CASTLE

Bunratty Castle, built in 1425 and restored in the 1950s, is the best-looking medieval fortress you can find in Ireland.

There are medieval banquets you can take part in—but be careful not to misbehave during the meal or you may be taken to the dungeon. Near the castle is the Folk Park that recreates a nineteenth century Irish village of 30 buildings.

Bunratty Castle

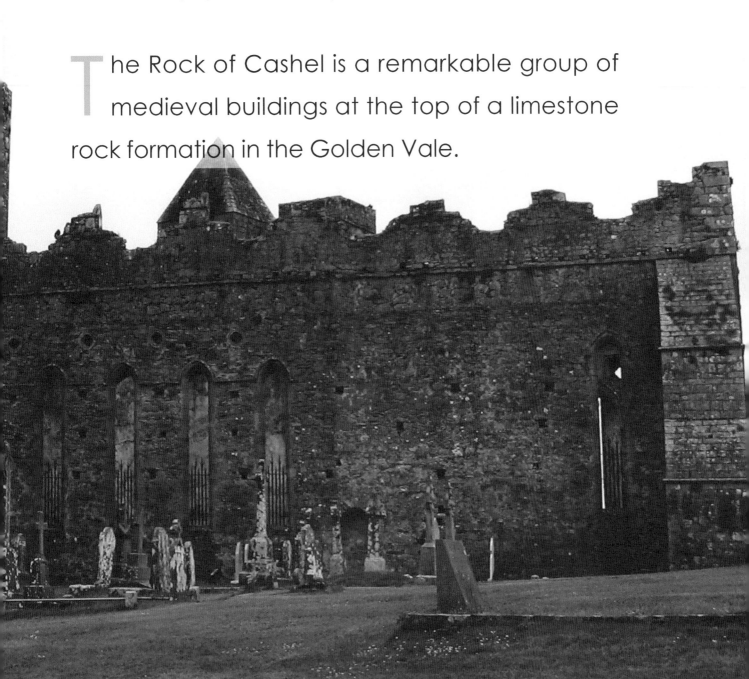

THE ROCK OF CASHEL

The Rock of Cashel is a remarkable group of medieval buildings at the top of a limestone rock formation in the Golden Vale.

The round tower dates to the twelfth century, the cathedral to the thirteenth century, and the castle to the fifteenth century. This is the most-visited heritage site in all of Ireland, and may have been the headquarters of the High Kings of Ireland in the period before the English invaded the island.

The Rock of Cashel

MEET THE IRISH!

No matter whom you meet in Ireland, the person is likely to smile. Irish people do a lot of smiling! They are friendly, welcoming, and generally happy to see you. And if you ask directions, they are likely to tell you a long story about the place you are trying to find, and not just directions for how to get there.

reland as a country has had its challenges and sorrows, and not every smiling person you meet is leading the ideal life of happiness. But for the Irish, having a ready smile is a good way to deal with a lot of life's challenges.

Temple Bar in Ireland

People you don't know may invite you to have a meal or a drink with them, and then insist on paying the bill! They will share their stories and ask about your plans, but not in an intrusive way.

Another thing you may notice is that Irish people say "Sorry" a lot. It is a way of avoiding conflict and anticipating your disappointment if something you wanted to see or eat is not available.

They even say "Sorry" to get your attention, when most North Americans would say "Excuse me". It takes a little getting used to, but it's a pleasing habit!

WHERE NEXT?

What other places in the world would you like to visit, and what other people would you like to meet? Baby Professor books like *What Can I See in Pompeii?*, *Where Should I Go in Egypt?* and *All the Sand in the Desert Can't Cover Up the Beauty of Saudi Arabia* can help you plan your next trip.

Pyramids in Egypt

Visit

www.BabyProfessorBooks.com

to download Free Baby Professor eBooks
and view our catalog of new and exciting
Children's Books

Made in the USA
Columbia, SC
25 May 2018